ENTERTAINMENT
AND
VIDEO GAMES

CONTEMPORARY ISSUES

XBOX 360

CONTEMPORARY ISSUES

ENTERTAINMENT
AND
VIDEO GAMES

ABBY BRYN

MASON CREST
PHILADELPHIA | MIAMI

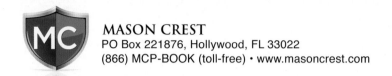

MASON CREST
PO Box 221876, Hollywood, FL 33022
(866) MCP-BOOK (toll-free) • www.masoncrest.com

Printed in the United States of America

First printing
9 8 7 6 5 4 3 2 1

Series ISBN: 978-1-4222-4538-5
Hardcover ISBN: 978-1-4222-4541-5
ebook ISBN: 978-1-4222-7266-4

Cataloging-in-Publication Data on file with the Library of Congress

Developed and Produced by National Highlights, Inc.
Cover and Interior Design: Torque Advertising + Design
Layout: Priceless Digital Media

Publisher's Note: Websites listed in this book were active at the time of publication. The publisher is not responsible for websites that have changed their address or discontinued operation since the date of publication. The publisher reviews and updates the websites each time the book is reprinted.

QR CODES AND LINKS TO THIRD-PARTY CONTENT

You may gain access to certain third-party content ("Third-Party Sites") by scanning and using the QR Codes that appear in this publication (the "QR Codes"). We do not operate or control in any respect any information, products, or services on such Third-Party Sites linked to by us via the QR Codes included in this publication, and we assume no responsibility for any materials you may access using the QR Codes. Your use of the QR Codes may be subject to terms, limitations, or restrictions set forth in the applicable terms of use or otherwise established by the owners of the Third-Party Sites. Our linking to such Third-Party Sites via the QR Codes does not imply an endorsement or sponsorship of such Third-Party Sites or the information, products, or services offered on or through the Third-Party Sites, nor does it imply an endorsement or sponsorship of this publication by the owners of such Third-Party Sites.

CONTENTS

KEY ICONS TO LOOK FOR:

Words to Understand: These words with their easy-to-understand definitions will increase the reader's understanding of the text while building vocabulary skills.

Sidebars: This boxed material within the main text allows readers to build knowledge, gain insights, explore possibilities, and broaden their perspectives by weaving together additional information to provide realistic and holistic perspectives.

Educational videos: Readers can view videos by scanning our QR codes, providing them with additional educational content to supplement the text. Examples include news coverage, moments in history, speeches, iconic sports moments, and much more!

Text-Dependent Questions: These questions send the reader back to the text for more careful attention to the evidence presented there.

Research Projects: Readers are pointed toward areas of further inquiry connected to each chapter. Suggestions are provided for projects that encourage deeper research and analysis.

Series Glossary of Key Terms: This back-of-the-book glossary contains terminology used throughout this series. Words found here increase the reader's ability to read and comprehend higher-level books and articles in this field.

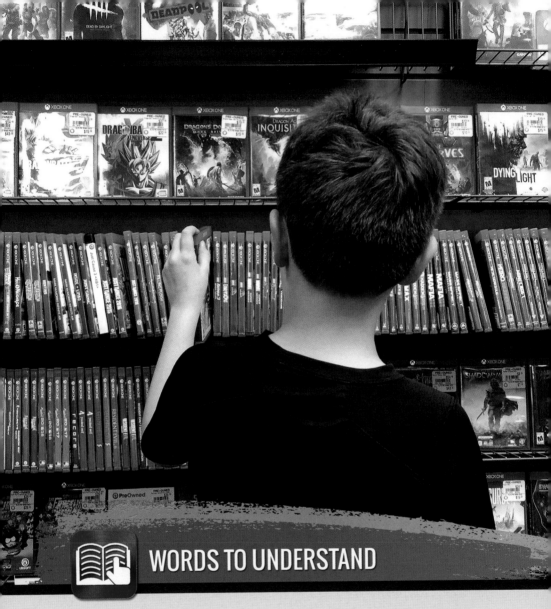

arcade—referring to a type of video game that is housed in a large cabinet, as well as a public location where these games can be played.

objectionable—referring to behavior that is met with social disapproval or is considered to be offensive or in poor taste.

pernicious—something that is harmful, often in a gradual or subtle way.

ENTERTAINMENT CONTROVERSY THROUGH HISTORY

For as long as there has been entertainment media, people have scrutinized it, expressing concern over content and whether there were **pernicious** elements in the work. The earliest such criticism goes back more than 2,500 years, when theatrical dramas began to take shape in ancient Greece. Since the early twentieth century, critics have focused on modern forms of entertainment, such as movies, television shows, popular music, and video games.

The film industry, for example, was still in its infancy during the early 1920s, when some critics began to charge that movies promoted immoral behavior. They protested against films that depicted sexuality, violence, and other things that some Americans considered **objectionable** at the time, including interracial relationships, homosexuality, and—though this may seem strange today—the depiction of women as strong, independent characters.

The backlash against the industry intensified when one of the biggest film stars of the time, Roscoe "Fatty" Arbuckle, was placed on trial for rape and manslaughter in 1921 and 1922. Although Arbuckle was acquitted, in 1922 a former politician named Will H. Hays was hired as head

"People who know how to make games need to start focusing on the task of making real life better for as many people as possible."[1]
—Jane McGonigal,
game designer and author

of the Motion Picture Association of America (MPAA), an organization of major American movie studios. Hays was ordered to improve the film industry's image, so he implemented a system of self-regulation, creating a code for filmmakers to follow that set certain guidelines and general policies for the industry. It was called the Motion Picture Production Code, although many people referred to it as the Hays Code.

The Hays Code banned profane language; nudity and sex scenes (including depictions of prostitution); and depictions of illegal drug use, adultery, and interracial relationships. It instructed film directors to make sure that violent stories were told in "good taste" and that criminals were not sympathetic figures. Films could not depict police officers, clergy members, or other authority figures as incompetent, silly, or villainous. (Exceptions could be made if the film were to make clear that such characters were exceptions to the rule, by contrasting them with authority figures who were portrayed in a more positive way.)

At first, adhering to the Hays Code was voluntary. Most movie studios obeyed the code so that their films would be approved by state censorship boards that reviewed movies before they were allowed to be released. In 1934, however, the MPAA created the Production Code Administration (PCA), which required all films to obtain a certificate of approval before being released.

Under the direction of PCA's head, Joseph I. Breen, the code was strictly enforced from 1934 until 1954. Breen demanded that studios rewrite or cut scenes that he found offensive or in violation of the code. However, in 1952 the US Supreme Court decided the landmark case *Joseph Burstyn Inc. v. Wilson*, ruling that motion pictures were protected under the First Amendment to the Constitution. That limited the effect of censorship both by state boards and the PCA.

Over time, movie producers became more emboldened to feature content that ran afoul of the code, sometimes releasing films without approval of the MPAA. One of the reasons that producers grew bolder was that television was making inroads into film audiences. Even though television had even more stringent censorship rules in place than the film code, it was more convenient to watch in the comfort of home. Producers feared that without more appealing content, the film industry would grow stagnant.

G	GENERAL AUDIENCES
	ALL AGES ADMITTED

PG	PARENTAL GUIDANCE SUGGESTED
SOME MATERIAL MAY NOT BE SUITABLE FOR CHILDREN	

PG-13	PARENTS STRONGLY CAUTIONED
SOME MATERIAL MAY BE INAPPROPRIATE FOR CHILDREN UNDER 13	

R	RESTRICTED
	UNDER 17 REQUIRES ACCOMPANYING PARENT OR ADULT GUARDIAN

NC-17	NO ONE 17 AND UNDER ADMITTED

In response to public concerns about violence and inappropriate content in movies, the Motion Picture Association of America (MPAA) adopted guidelines for filmmakers. The MPAA eventually created a guide to help viewers choose films that were appropriate for their families. The current MPAA ratings range from G (suitable for everyone) to NC-17 (no admission for anyone under age seventeen).

The code was finally abandoned during the 1960s, with the MPAA in 1968 replacing it with a rating system, still used, that would declare films as appropriate for certain age groups. For example, a G-rated film would be appropriate for viewers of all ages, while an R-rated film would be restricted, and viewers under age sixteen or seventeen would be required to be accompanied by an adult.

Although the rating system proved to be less restrictive, it still has problems. The MPAA has been criticized for the ways in which it treats sex and violence when rating movies. Critics have pointed out that, according to the MPAA's website, films with strong sexual content are four times as likely to receive an NC-17 (no admission to anyone under age seventeen) rating than are extremely violent films.

In recent years, horror movies like It: Chapter Two, Zombieland 2, Annabelle Comes Home, *and* Us *have been among the most popular, and profitable, films in the United States, despite gory scenes and shocking violence.*

RATING COMICS AND GAMES

Film wasn't the only entertainment medium that implemented codes and standards of permissible depictions. Comic books also faced controversy during the 1950s, and that industry developed its own code. Like the Hays Code of the 1920s, the Comics Code was formed due to fear that comic books would become a target of government regulation. The Comics Code Authority (CCA), which oversaw the code, could not prevent comic books that violated its principles from being produced. However, many stores would only sell comic books that included the CCA's seal of approval.

During the 1950s, psychologist Frederic Wertham wrote books and articles asserting that the violence in comic books caused young people to get into trouble with the law. His testimony before Congress in 1954 resulted in the creation of the Comics Code Authority.

That is why entertainment media companies often adhere to such rules and guidelines. Whether they are making movies, video games, comic books, music, or television shows, businesses can decide not to sell the products if they do not follow their respective rating systems, which are meant to reassure parents that the products will not be inappropriate for their children.

The Comics Code wound up having major effects on various comic publishers. Some cancelled titles, while others simply stopped publishing altogether. Sometimes, the Comics Code was misused to prevent stories that featured Black or female leading characters. However, by the 1960s publishers began to push back against the code, and it diminished in strictness and relevance. The Comics Code finally ended in 2011, when the last two publishers who observed it—DC Comics and Archie Comics—cut ties.

During the 1980s, a major issue of concern for gaming occurred in the realm of tabletop games. Dungeons & Dragons, a popular role-playing game, faced massive criticism from religious organizations and conservative parent groups. Some of this opposition was fueled by misunderstandings, as in the 1979 case of James Egbert, a college student who disappeared and eventually committed suicide. Stories about Egbert that noted his involvement in Dungeons & Dragons, as well as the fact that he had tried to commit suicide in maintenance tunnels under the Michigan State University campus, inspired numerous novels in which characters lose touch with reality because of playing role-playing games. One of those novels, *Mazes and Monsters* (1981), was later turned into a TV movie that starred a young Tom Hanks as an obsessive game player who goes nuts on the streets of New York City. Another novel, *Hobgoblin* (1981), ended with the game player involved in a bloody slaughter. Those books and others facilitated the urban myth about role-playing gamers becoming dangerously detached from reality.

The controversy over Dungeons & Dragons continued into the 1990s, with accusations that the game encouraged rape, suicide, and satanic worship. However, independent investigations found no real-life examples of those behaviors. In fact, some studies found that young people who played Dungeons & Dragons were less likely to experience suicidal tendencies or thoughts than those who did not.

"Congress should fund research on the effects that violent video games have on young minds."[2]

—*Barack Obama, former US president*

Scan here to learn more about the early video game Tennis for Two.

VIDEO GAMES

Video games have been popular for decades. The very first one that was shown to the public for demonstration was *Bertie the Brain*, a tic-tac-toe video game created for the 1950 Canadian National Exhibition. *Tennis for Two* was another early video game, created in the late 1950s. *Spacewar!,* created in 1962, could be played on the mainframe computers owned by many colleges and scientific institutions, and it exposed more people to video games.

The first commercial **arcade** video game console was *Pong*, created in 1972. A simple ping-pong game, *Pong* was created by Nolan Bushnell and Ted Dabney, who would go on to found a video game company called Atari. That same year, the Magnavox Odyssey, the first commercially successful home video game console, was released.

The Odyssey could be hooked up to a television set, allowing simple games to be played at home. Soon, other home game consoles were being developed and sold.

In 1977, the Atari 2600 console popularized the idea of a computer system that could play games stored on cartridges.

 ## POLITICAL VIEWS ON VIOLENT VIDEO GAMES

The subject of video game violence has evolved in a lot of ways, and politicians from both major parties have at times attacked the industry for what they view as excessive violence. In 1993, controversy over violence in games like *Mortal Kombat* led to congressional hearings. The hearing in the US Senate was spearheaded by Democrats Joe Lieberman and Herb Kohl. In response, game publishers created the Entertainment Software Rating Board (ESRB) in 1994 to help parents understand the content of specific games.

After the April 1999 Columbine school shooting in Colorado, Speaker of the House Newt Gingrich, a Republican, claimed that violence in video games, movies, and television had "undermined the core values of civility."[3] President Bill Clinton, a Democrat, asked the Federal Trade Commission (FTC) and the Department of Justice (DOJ) to determine whether firms in the movie, music recording, and video game industries were marketing violent materials to young people.

In 2005, the California legislature passed a law that would have banned the sale or rental of violent video games to people under the age of eighteen. Game

That made the system more flexible, as new games could be developed each year. Since then, video games have improved with each generation, Their concepts have become more diverse, and their visuals have become clearer and more realistic. In the late 1980s, the Japanese company Nintendo gained a large share of the home video game market with the introduction of the Nintendo Entertainment System, its own cartridge-based console. Other companies also competed for the home gaming market, including Sega,

publishers quickly filed a lawsuit that blocked the law from taking effect. After years of legal challenges, in 2011 the US Supreme Court ruled (by a 7–2 vote) that the law was an unconstitutional violation of the First Amendment.

As mass shootings continued, in 2013 President Barack Obama, a Democrat, introduced a plan to reduce gun violence. One element of that plan was for the federal government to fund research into the effects of video game violence. However, over the next few years, Congress and the states actually reduced funding for mental health services and research into the causes of violence.

In a meeting on school safety, held at the White House just weeks after a school shooting in Parkland, Florida, killed fourteen students and three staff members in February of 2018, President Donald Trump spoke about the issue. "The video games, the movies, the internet stuff is so violent. It's so incredible," said Trump. "It's hard to believe that, at least for a percentage—and maybe it's a small percentage of children—this doesn't have a negative impact on their thought process. But these things are really violent."[4]

Sony, and Microsoft. Sony has been highly successful with its PlayStation line of consoles.

Advancements in computer graphics have also created more sophisticated and immersive video games. For example, the 2018 video game *Red Dead Redemption 2* went above and beyond to feature realism to the smallest detail. Yet, as video games grow more advanced, there are also

In the 1980s, some people were concerned that role-playing games like Dungeons & Dragons contributed to mental illness or suicide. However, these fears turned out to be unfounded.

The Atari Video Computer System (later called Atari 2600) was one of the first popular home video game consoles. It was introduced in 1977. Unlike previous home video games, the Atari could play a variety of different games that were saved on cartridges, with new games being developed each year.

downsides. More realistic themes often mean more adult situations, such as sexual content or violence, or the content can be so immersive that the player finds it hard for them to pull themselves away from the game.

Perhaps the earliest mainstream controversy that video games faced was related to the ways that violent video games could affect children. The 1976 arcade game *Death Race* required players to run over gremlins in their vehicles. The news media, including the television show *60 Minutes*, the *New York Times*, and the Associated Press, wrote articles that criticized the game for its morbid content. In the 1980s, US Surgeon General C. Everett Koop suggested that there might be a connection between video games and children's mental health. However, studies ultimately found that evidence for such a link was not conclusive.

With technical advancement comes a significantly greater degree of realism, and with realism comes a greater ability to depict real-world concepts. Video games on Atari

The Entertainment Software Ratings Board (ESRB) was created during the 1990s to advise parents about the suitability of video games for young people. Today, ESRB ratings range from E (everyone) to AO (adults only).

consoles from the 1970s had relatively poor or simplistic graphics. Even when a game showed a spaceship blowing up or depicted human-on-human violence, it was typically very hard to tell what was actually happening. But as video game graphics became more realistic, so did violence, with games depicting blood spurting or other gory scenes in bright pixels. Games like *Mortal Kombat* and *Night Trap*, both released in 1992, became so controversial, due to their violent content, that Congress held hearings about inappropriate content in video games, which led to the creation of the Entertainment Software Rating Board

(ESRB), which is intended to advise consumers—particularly parents—about video games. Despite concern from lawyers, parents, teachers, politicians, and others, game publishers continue to promote violent video games.

RATING TELEVISION AND MUSIC

The television industry struggled for years to find a way to warn viewers about violent or sexual content. Federal law prohibits "obscene, indecent and profane content" from being broadcast on the radio or TV.[5] For many years, network executives only aired mature programming late at night, although still during the hours of "prime time," when networks charge the most money for advertising. This meant that mature programming was hitting the airwaves as early as 10:00 PM—a time when some young people were still tuned in.

Technological advancements during the late 1990s made it easier to restrict young viewers from seeing certain types of content. TV manufacturers began installing devices called "V-chips" in televisions. These devices enabled parents to program their televisions to block specific shows that they felt were inappropriate for their families. A rating system for television shows was developed, with programs designated "TV-Y" or "TV-G" being suitable for young children. For older audiences, there is "TV-PG," which means that the content may be unsuitable for younger children, and encourages parental guidance; "TV-14," which warns parents that the programming contains material that may be unsuitable for children ages fourteen and younger;

and "TV-MA," which means the programming should only be viewed by adults.

For many years, the recording industry was opposed to a parental advisory system. During the mid-1980s, concern about offensive song lyrics led to the formation of the Parents' Music Resource Center (PMRC) by Tipper Gore and Susan Baker. Both were connected to high-ranking political figures: Gore was the wife of Senator (and later Vice President) Al Gore, a Democrat from Tennessee, while Baker's husband, James, was at the time the secretary of the US Treasury. The organization made a list of songs that it felt was inappropriate, known as the "Filthy Fifteen," that included hits by such stars as Madonna, Cyndi Lauper, Mötley Crüe, Def Leppard, Prince, and other recording artists.

In September of 1985, the Senate held hearings about the issue. Mrs. Gore and Mrs. Baker were among those who testified, suggesting that record companies should put parental-advisory labels on albums that contained sexually explicit or violent lyrics. They also wanted all song lyrics to be printed and issued with records so that parents could read them. Country star John Denver, rock composer Frank Zappa, and Twisted Sister lead singer Dee Snyder testified against the labels, calling them censorship.

Ultimately, the Recording Industry Association of America (RIAA) voluntarily chose to put advisory labels on certain releases that contained explicit or violent lyrics. Some retailers will not sell music that carries those labels.

TEXT-DEPENDENT QUESTIONS

1. What was the nickname for the Motion Picture Production Code?
2. What 1976 game attracted controversy for its depiction of violence?
3. What is the line of Sony video game consoles called?

 RESEARCH PROJECTS

Video game controversies were fairly common in the 1990s, especially because little was known about violence's effect on children and how little regulation the industry had on content. Find a 1990s video game, not covered in this section, that attracted controversy for its depiction of violence. Write a two-page paper.

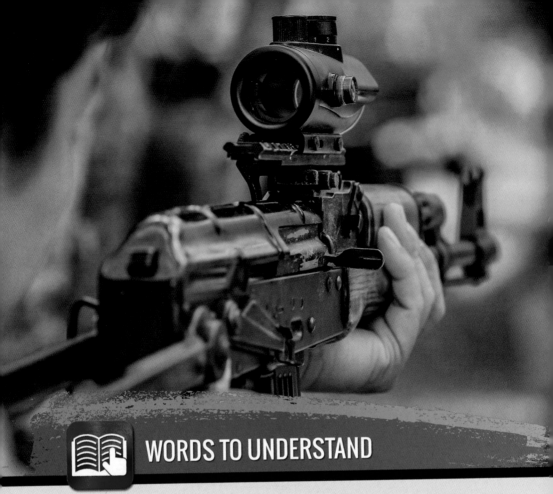

WORDS TO UNDERSTAND

desensitize—to make someone feel less shock, sensitivity, or distress about something, such as cruelty, violence, or suffering.

methodology—a group of rules or established procedures used to research or investigate something.

propaganda—information, especially of a biased or misleading nature, used to promote or publicize a particular political cause or point of view.

white phosphorus munitions—a military weapon; the material is set aflame by contact with the air and is known to cause severe bubbling of the skin and damage to the liver and kidneys, putting a person at risk of total organ failure.

DO VIDEO GAMES INFLUENCE VIOLENCE?

CHAPTER 2

Politicians have often pushed a narrative that video games are responsible for multiple mass shootings and violence in general. The 1993 video game *Doom*, for example, has often been linked to the Columbine High School massacre in April of 1999, with rumors that the two shooters had trained for their attack by creating a map in the game that was modeled after their high school's hallways, classrooms, and cafeteria spaces. The deadly attack left fifteen people dead and twenty-one injured. At a time when school shootings and other mass shootings were relatively rare, the attack shocked the nation and focused new attention on violence in video games.

Tragically, mass shootings are much more common today than they were twenty years ago. Many people blame video games and other violence in the media for this increase. After a surge in mass shootings, even the president of the United States weighed in. "I'm hearing more and more people say the level of violence on video games is really shaping young people's thoughts," Donald Trump told Florida's attorney general in March 2018. He later tweeted,

"Video game violence & glorification must be stopped—it is creating monsters!"[6]

Although the subject of video game violence and its effect on children has been studied for more than forty years, the debate is still going strong. The following essays examine two sides of this controversial topic.

Surveillance video shows Eric Harris (left) and Dylan Klebold in the cafeteria at Columbine High School during their April 1999 shooting spree. Some people speculated that video game violence may have contributed to the horrible school shooting.

Scan here for some concerns about video games.

VIDEO GAMES ENCOURAGE VIOLENCE

In a review of more than forty years of studies related to the links between violence in the media and violence and aggression in people, psychologist Craig A. Anderson observed that the research suggests that the interactive nature of video games could result in violent video games having a stronger negative effect on people than any other entertainment medium. Anderson, a professor at Iowa State University, is considered one of the foremost researchers into the effects of violent video games on children. He points out that video game violence tends to go far beyond what is considered acceptable in television shows or movies, and notes that some games reward players for killing police officers or innocent bystanders, or other criminal behavior.

"Identifying with an aggressor has been shown to increase the likelihood of adopting aggressive behaviors and attitudes," writes Anderson. "In violent video games, the player strongly identifies with (and usually takes the role of) the aggressor. The aggressive central character is usually glorified and portrayed as heroic and, in recent years, the portrayal of aggressive characters in video games has become increasingly realistic (Gentile et al., 2007). For these reasons, identification with violent/aggressive characters may be a key way that video games impact children."[7]

A study conducted by the American Psychiatric Association (APA) in 2005 concluded that exposure to violent media resulted in hostility, suspicion, aggression, and other responses. It also found that exposure to sexual

 ## USING VIOLENCE TO SELL

Some video games have been created or marketed with the controversy over violence in mind. As part of a marketing campaign for the 1998 video game *Thrill Kill,* game publisher Electronic Arts sent demonstration discs of the game to reviewers. Some criticized the game because of its gratuitous violence and sexual content. EA ultimately canceled the game when it received an "Adult Only" rating from the Entertainment Software Rating Board, fearing that its release would create too much negative publicity for the company.

violence in media caused people to become **desensitized** to violence in real life, making them more likely to commit violence against women and express general anti-woman sentiments. One of the APA's recommendations at the end of this study was that video game creators should make a point of reducing the amount and severity of violence in video games marketed to children.

The American Academy of Pediatrics (AAP), an association for doctors who specialize in caring for children, has also issued a strong statement against video game violence. "Parents should be mindful of what shows their children watch and which games they play," the organization noted in its journal *Pediatrics*. "Young children (under the age of six years) need to be protected from virtual violence. Parents should understand that young children do not always distinguish fantasy from reality. Cartoon violence can seem very real, and it can have detrimental

About a dozen years later, however, EA's position on controversy seemed to have changed. Their marketing campaign for the 2011 video game *Dead Space 2*, an alien-shooting game, featured video clips on Facebook of mothers watching violent scenes from the game and discussing how disgusting and vile the game was. EA spun their dislike of the violence as a positive for teenage gamers, with the tagline "Your mom hates *Dead Space 2*."

effects. Furthermore, first-person shooter games, in which killing others is the central theme, are not appropriate for any children."[8]

Unfortunately, little has changed. In 2015, a follow-up study conducted by the American Psychological Association examined the relationship between aggression and playing violent video games. The study found that young people who played violent video games showed greater aggression than those who did not. It also found that the subjects experienced lessened empathy and sensitivity toward aggression. However, the APA did note that in spite of these findings, it could not find conclusive evidence that would suggest a connection between playing violent video games and criminal violence.

"The goal is to make it such a negative thing that the retailers won't carry it. This thing hasn't really reached critical mass as a [public relations] problem yet; that's what I'm trying to do. Nobody shoots anybody in the face unless you're a hit man or a video gamer."[9]
—Former attorney Jack Thompson

In February 2018, Nikolas Cruz killed seventeen people and injured seventeen others at Marjorie Stoneman Douglas High School in Parkland, Florida. Police discovered that Cruz regularly played violent video games, sometimes for up to fifteen hours at a time.

There has been discussion about whether the resulting increase in aggressive behavior is the product of the violence in video games, or whether the competitive nature of certain video games is the reason (or a reason) for the increase. A study conducted by Nicholas Lee Carnagey sought to answer that question and found that, when comparing violent sports video games (such as *NFL Blitz*, *MLB Slugfest*, and *NHL Hits*, which typically contained more violent content than competing games of their respective sports) to nonviolent sports video games, the former category of video game showed heightened aggression. Another study of real-world sports games found that people participating in high-contact sports, such as football and basketball, showed a higher level of aggression when compared to low-contact sports such as track and baseball.

More recently, sociologists have begun to analyze how sexist depictions of women in media influence real-world views of women. One recent study determined that such sexism can result in a reduced degree of empathy toward women. Though the study's authors noted that there was no direct game effect, they argued that the interactions of

Games like Call of Duty: Modern Warfare *have been criticized for allowing players to use deadly weapons without providing a context for the difficult decision to use such weapons, or their devastating effects on victims in the real world.*

various aspects of the game and sexist themes provided adequate evidence to claim a causal effect. This study has received criticism, however, with some scholars suggesting the **methodology** used may have been flawed.

One related issue regarding violence in video games is the way that some games seem to glorify the idea of real-world violence. These games tend to depict war in a fun and/or exciting way. While most are meant to produce an entertaining experience for players, some products have served as **propaganda** that encourages young people to join the military. This is particularly true of some popular first-person shooter games, such as *Call of Duty*, *Medal of Honor,* and others.

Call of Duty and *Medal of Honor* are more grounded in reality, typically depicting events taken from history (such as World War II) or at least based on real-world events. The 2019 edition of *Call of Duty: Modern Warfare* attracted controversy due to its depiction of the use of **white phosphorus munitions**. When a player hits level fifty-one (achieved by a kill streak), the ability to rain this deadly weapon down on enemies is unlocked. However, the Geneva Convention considers the military use of such munitions against humans to be a war crime, so some people criticized its inclusion in the game. The full implications of using horrific weapons of war, such as white phosphorus munitions or even nuclear weapons, are rarely explained or placed into context within the larger story of the game. They are simply another way to eliminate enemies, and players never come to understand or appreciate the horrors of such weapons.

In a discussion by American soldiers about how war is depicted in video games, one soldier noted that combat was often unrealistic. He mentioned how in the games, enemy soldiers often stand out in the open, making them easy targets for the player to shoot. Also, while these games have realistic aspects, there is no real sense of danger for the players. When players are killed, they simply respawn and continue to fight. One such game is *America's Army*, created by the Pentagon in 2002 to encourage recruitment into the armed forces. Author Hamza Shaban calls it "hypocrisy, that a game meant to teach people about the service fails to convey a sense of loss or carnal gore."[10]

Others feel that video games desensitize the players to violence by glorifying war and trivializing the decision to kill. A game called *Kuma/War* has released over 120 missions, some of which are based on real-life military encounters or scenarios. Episode 107 depicted the May 2011 Navy SEAL raid in Pakistan that resulted in the death of terrorist leader Osama bin Laden, the mastermind of the al-Qaeda attacks against the United States that occurred on September 11, 2001. The game gave players the chance to pull the trigger on bin Laden and others at the compound—possibly including his children or family members. Another episode of the game featured Libyan rebels attacking the city of Sirte and killing the late Libyan dictator Muammar Gaddafi.

The Grand Theft Auto series of games is extremely popular, but the games have been criticized for their over-the-top violence, as well as demeaning depictions of women.

"Today's video games heavily contribute to the prominent military culture of the United States," writes Jai Mediratta in an editorial in the *Daily Nebraskan*. "In addition, the video games trivialize the realities of war. They convolute the meaning of death and fail to recognize the actual objectives of real-time war missions. Video games glorify the mindless slaughter done under the guise of heroism, while simultaneously desensitizing civilians to one of the most destructive forces of mankind. War is not a game—war is a curse."[11]

Since 2018, *Fortnite* has been among the world's most popular video games, particularly among young teenagers.

The game is far more colorful and less serious than other video games, so some people feel that the violence does not affect young players. Dr. Michael Rich, a pediatrician and the founder of the Center on Media and Child Health, disagrees. "When comparing *Fortnite* to other popular shooter games, such as *Halo, Grand Theft Auto*, and *Call of Duty, Fortnite's* graphics indeed seem cartoonish, with less graphic carnage and gore when players kill others. Interestingly, the level of detail is amped up when it comes to weapons, as players can obtain a varied arsenal, from battleaxes to assault rifles. *Fortnite*'s combination of weapon glorification and cartoonish violence is concerning as the player sees the world through a lens that values weaponry, but downplays and makes abstract the damage those weapons cause. Each bloodless death of another player (not just a computer-generated avatar) is simply one mission accomplished, one step closer to winning—time to hit the next target!"[12]

Although some defenders of video games like to claim that the link between them and real-world violence is not proven, psychologist Craig Anderson disagrees. According to his review of the scientific literature, the overwhelming number of studies clearly indicate such a link. "Some studies have yielded nonsignificant video game effects, just as some smoking studies failed to find a significant link to lung cancer," writes Anderson. "But when one combines all relevant empirical studies using meta-analytic techniques, five separate effects emerge with considerable consistency.

*The popular game **Fortnite** is highly competitive, particularly the "Battle Royale" element in which players use a variety of weapons in a fight to the death.*

Violent video games are significantly associated with: increased aggressive behavior, thoughts, and affect; increased physiological arousal; and decreased prosocial (helping) behavior."[13]

VIDEO GAMES DO NOT ENCOURAGE VIOLENCE

In 2014, Patrick M. Markey, a psychology professor at Villanova University, and his wife, Charlotte, a professor at Rutgers University, conducted a study of violent video games. They compared thirty years of FBI data on crime rates to the dates of video game releases. The researchers expected to see an increase in violence around the times when games like *Doom* or *Grand Theft Auto* became available. What they found, however, was that homicides and aggravated assaults actually dropped when violent games were released.

Although the researchers warned of the need for caution when using correlative data, they pointed out that even after making adjustments to reflect periods when murder and assault rates are traditionally higher (such as during the summer), and periods when game sales naturally rise (such as before certain holidays), there remained a statistically significant negative relationship between violence and video games.

"The notion that all, or even most, individuals who play violent video games will inevitably become aggressive may be unwarranted," stated the study's conclusion. "Instead, it appears that it is crucial to consider various personality traits of the person playing the violent video game when predicting whether the violent video games will have adverse effects."[14]

The Markeys suggest that their findings could indicate that violent video games serve as a catharsis for people who are more prone to violence, but the data also indicates that video games are merely a distraction from the real world. While violent people may find enjoyment in violent games, the games by themselves do not appear to cause people to become violent. The Markeys also note that it's "quite a leap" to say that violent video games lead to mass shootings like those in Dayton, El Paso, Parkland, Las Vegas, or Columbine. "Given the number of youths who regularly engage in violent video game play and the general concern regarding this media, [such shootings] would be a regular occurrence," concluded their study. "And yet, daily reports of mass violence are not reported. It appears that the vast majority of individuals exposed to violent video games do not become violent in the 'real world.'"[15]

Studies like Dr. Craig A. Anderson's have been criticized as being misleading. Some experts have suggested that Anderson and the American Psychological Association misrepresented what the scientific literature had to say about violence in video games, and engaged in cherry-picking to avoid studies that contradicted their conclusions. In 2013, an international group of 228 media scholars, psychologists, and criminologists sent an open letter to the American Psychological Association, asking it to reconsider its position on the effects of violence in the media. The signers found the evidence to be too inclusive to justify the APA's definitive stance. "We express the concern that the APA's previous (2005) policy statement delineated several strong conclusions on the basis of inconsistent or weak evidence," noted the letter. "Research subsequent to that 2005 statement has provided even stronger evidence that some of the assertions in it cannot be supported.... Youth violence in the United States and elsewhere has plummeted to forty-year lows, not risen as would have been expected if the 2005 APA resolution were accurate."[16]

In 2013, a study analyzed the reasons why classic prosocial (i.e., positive) video games, such as *Animal Crossing*, *Minecraft*, and *Gone Home*, promoted prosocial behavior in real life, while classic violent video games did not have any effect. The authors of the study wished to determine whether the reason was because of the games used (specifically, whether more modern violent video games would have an effect that classic ones do not). After their research was finished, the study authors determined that no link could be found between a reduction in prosocial behavior and the playing of modern violent

"Correlation doesn't mean causation. But we haven't just looked at sales of games and violent crimes. We have taken into account trends in the data. We remove stuff that typically happens, like a spike in murders during summer and high sales of games near the holidays, and it's still negative.
To me, what is most amazing is that is never positive. It is always statistically negative."[17]

—Patrick Markey,
psychology professor and author

video games. They also made a point of saying that due to the public interest of studies on violent video games and their effects on people, it is important for speculation to undergo rigorous testing rather than being taken on its face.

When it comes to violence in media, most of what a person finds is gratuitous. However, that does not mean violence cannot be depicted in such a way that does not glamorize violence. This is sometimes seen in video games about war, depicting people attempting to escape violence, people who commit violence as a survival method, and soldiers trying to deal with the trauma and conflict of being perpetrators of violence.

The 2012 game *Spec Ops: The Line* is an example of this type of story. In one cut scene, the player's character, Captain Walker, orders a strike with white phosphorus munitions against enemy troops over the objections of another character. After the strike, the characters realize that they have accidentally killed civilians as well as enemy soldiers. That leads into the theme of the game, which depicts the soldiers gradually coming to understand war crimes and the horrors of combat.

Other games also depict civilians in the midst of a war. A game called *This War of Mine* lets the players control civilians who are trying to survive as combat rages around them. Survival entails maintaining the characters' mental and physical health by keeping them fed, hydrated, and warm, and by keeping their morale up. Players are frequently challenged on their morale, often having to

Researchers have found that certain games, such as Minecraft, promote cooperative behavior among young people.

resort to theft or possibly violence toward other people who are just trying to survive. The violence never feels very good for the player, which itself serves as an incentive to avoid violence whenever possible.

The *Metal Gear* franchise tends toward an antiwar perspective, touching upon war-related topics and contextualizing them as damaging. The games do not depict villains as simply being villains for the sake of it, but rather explaining their reason for being villains as a source of trauma, as well as depicting the protagonist as being a part of something insidious or underhanded. The game also works well in that players often need not kill any regular enemies. One example in the series, *Metal Gear Solid 4: Guns of the Patriots*, is the only one that allows players to actually go through the entire game without having to kill a single person. The game even rewards players at the end for having avoided killing. Going through the game can be difficult if the player chooses not to kill anyone, as they have to either avoid or incapacitate the soldiers.

Another example from this franchise is *Metal Gear Rising: Revengeance*. The game stands out due to the ability of its protagonist, Raiden, to cut people and robots into pieces using his samurai sword, which is, as one can expect, pretty gory. However, players can equip the protagonist with a wooden sword, thus giving them the ability to knock the character out instead of killing him. The game presents combat in a negative light, with the antagonist being a politician who encourages attacks in order to spur war for the sake of profit.

Undertale is an interesting case of how violence is depicted. Not only can players kill characters, but there is even an ending that involves killing every single character in the game. While that may seem gratuitous, the game presents the decision to do so as anything but that. When a character is killed—especially when the player-character is explicitly looking to kill all of the characters in the game—the game makes it very clear that they are a villain, a deviant, a fiend. Characters will comment on awful things they've done, especially if they kill major characters. The game even tries to discourage players from trying to kill; the so-called "genocide run" is intentionally very tedious and difficult to win. Overall, this strategy is much less popular among game players than the alternative, coined as the "pacifist route." *Undertale* allows players to not kill a single character, and arguably that is a more interesting way to play the game. There is a different way to pacify each enemy, so the game becomes a series of logic puzzles. Not only does it offer this, it opens a number of story-based paths, where players may get a lot more detail about different characters in emotional scenes. Although the creator, Toby Fox, denies pushing players one way or the other, the game certainly feels like it is best played by killing no one. If a player chooses to kill even one enemy, they will miss out on the good ending as a result.

TEXT-DEPENDENT QUESTIONS

What video game faced controversy for allowing players to use white phosphorus munitions? Why?

What is an example of a video game that offers players the ability to beat it without killing anyone?

What are two approaches that a player can take in the game *Undertale*?

RESEARCH PROJECTS

Ever since violence in video games became a hot-button issue for politicians, the video game industry has made a point of self-regulation in order to avoid government regulation. It has accomplished this through the Entertainment Software Rating Board, with ratings modified over time in an attempt to offer more ratings types, such as the introduction of E10+ for everyone ages 10 and up to slot in between the E (for Everyone) rating and the T (for Teen) rating. How satisfied are parents and/or politicians? Write a two-page paper.

MMORPG—Massively Multiplayer Online Role-Playing Game, an online game in which a large number of people play together in a shared space.

post-traumatic stress disorder (PTSD)—a condition that involves experiencing mental and emotional stress due to injury or severe psychological shock, often with difficulty tuning out of what triggers symptoms.

venous thromboembolism—a condition wherein a blood clot is formed in the veins of the arms, legs, or groin and circulates, getting lodged in the lungs.

CAN ENTERTAINMENT MEDIA HELP PHYSICAL AND MENTAL HEALTH?

CHAPTER 3

One of the most pressing concerns that society faces today is related to exercise and health. Since the 1960s, the average weight of Americans has risen significantly. That has resulted in serious health problems for many people. The more weight a person gains, the greater their risk of heart disease, high blood pressure, stroke, diabetes, infertility, gallbladder disease, and osteoarthritis, as well as certain forms of cancer. The Centers for Disease Control and Prevention (CDC) has determined that being overweight/obese, combined with physical inactivity, is the second leading cause of preventable deaths in the United States, behind only tobacco use.

For most Americans, the way to combat obesity is not complicated: eat less, and exercise more. But the solution, while simple to identify, is not easy to implement in a nation that is inundated by prepared foods and prone to sedentary work habits and limited physical activity. Many American children prefer to consume junk food, watch television, or play video games than to eat sensibly and participate in sports or similar activities. A drastic increase in the amount of "screen time" has contributed to the problem. A recent survey by Common Sense Media found that teenagers spend an average of more than forty hours a week sitting in front of some type of screen. Those hours spent in front of a television, computer, or game screen mean less time devoted to physical activity. And the more sedentary children are, the more likely they are to be overweight, now and in the future.

Young people spend approximately forty hours a week on their phones or in front of other electronic devices with screens, such as televisions, computers, or tablets.

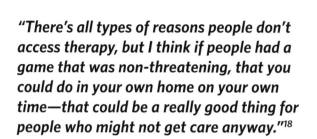

"There's all types of reasons people don't access therapy, but I think if people had a game that was non-threatening, that you could do in your own home on your own time—that could be a really good thing for people who might not get care anyway."[18]

—Christina Lelon, specialist in elder care

Efforts have been made to try to curb the increase in screen time, though they have not been effective. Many forms of media, and particularly video games, seem to encourage extended use, and younger people without the ability to properly self-moderate have found it difficult to determine how much time playing games is a responsible amount. Some companies have attempted to mitigate the screen-time issue by incorporate healthy practices and activities into their games.

The following essays examine two sides of the issue of whether video games are inherently unhealthy or whether they can provide some benefits for mental and physical health.

VIDEO GAMES IMPROVE MENTAL AND PHYSICAL HEALTH

Since the 1980s, there has been a boom in exercise-based and exercise-beneficial video games. For example, Nintendo's *World Class Track Meet* (1988) used a special running pad controller attached to the Nintendo Entertainment System. *Dance Dance Revolution* (1999) was released both in an arcade form and for home consoles, enabling players to dance and move using a special dance mat controller. There were also several gaming systems in the 1980s and 1990s that could be hooked up to an exercise bike or a rowing machine.

The release of Nintendo's Wii console in 2006, and the introduction of its wireless motion-sensitive controllers and balance board, encouraged greater movement among gamers. (Microsoft's Kinect, released in 2010, was a similar motion-sensing device that enabled dance and activity games on the Xbox 360 platform.) One game that brought exercise to the forefront was *Wii Sports,* which utilized the motion controls to enable gamers to play baseball, golf, and tennis, and to box or bowl. This game was praised for how easy the online sports were to play and how they required activity to be successful. The game was even used to help encourage exercise in elderly people and those in physical therapy, though the game was played by people of all ages, including children.

Nintendo would later expand upon this concept with *Wii Fit*, an exercise game that allows players to use both the Wii

Games like Dance Dance Revolution *subtly encourage exercise because players must move their bodies and be active in order to succeed.*

Balance Board and Wii Remote to do such activities as yoga and aerobics. One of the functions of the *Wii Fit* was that it could measure players' weight and track their weight loss or fitness accomplishments. More recently, Nintendo released *Ring Fit Adventure* for the Nintendo Switch. That game uses a pair of accessories that require players to exercise as they progress through what is a more traditional adventure game than their other sports games. There also have been video games designed around managing one's diet, though those kinds of games were most popular on the Nintendo DS and Nintendo Wii.

VIDEO GAMES AND SCIENTIFIC SCENARIOS

Video games have been used for various simulations and tests of real-work scenarios. They provide researchers and experts the ability to experiment or observe what would happen in a controlled environment much more easily, and less expensively, than such research would cost if done in the field.

One game inadvertently helped scientists better understand how infectious diseases, such as the novel coronavirus that appeared in early 2020, can spread so quickly. The popular MMORPG *World of Warcraft* developed a glitch in the software that caused a poison technique, intended to be limited to the area the person using the technique was in, to spread through the game. The poison could not harm the nonplayable characters,

Nintendo has also been a particularly strong proponent of responsible gaming. Some of its games actually tell players who have been involved in the game for a long period of time to take a break. Other companies have also implemented incentives to stop playing certain games for a period of time. In *The World Ends with You*, from publisher Square Enix, characters would gain experience bonuses for every day they didn't play. That gave players an incentive to not bury their noses in the game for hours at a time. The other is *Final Fantasy XIV*, a massively multiplayer online role-playing game **(MMORPG)**. It has a system called "rested experience," which benefits players while they are offline. Other MMORPGs also feature this, such as *World of Warcraft*.

but it would still infect them, causing them to become carriers who, in turn, could infect players.

The ways that this infection spread had many similarities to the spread of a pandemic in the real world, and the model of player behavior matched up as well. Uninfected players tried to escape to less populated areas; some characters would bravely try to treat the disease and became infected as a result; some players would attempt to scam others by selling fake cures; and there were even people who tried to spread the disease for fun. All of these virtual-world actions matched how people acted in a real-world pandemic, and helped to inform scientists about how to prepare for future ones.[19]

Video games have been useful in treating **post-traumatic stress disorder (PTSD)** and have been used by the US military to treat soldiers suffering with that problem. "One of the troubling symptoms of PTSD is an inability to concentrate because their attention is too focused on potential threats," writes Melissa Glim.

"This can lead to difficulties in executive functioning and the ability to complete tasks. Computer programs designed to retrain the attention system have been found to be useful in populations with various anxiety disorders, who are primed to pay too much attention to perceived threats."[20]

One study of video games and PTSD tested soldiers from the Israeli Defense Force and the US Army. They were tasked with playing an interactive system where they had to press a key to match either words or photographs.

Scan here to learn more about how video games can improve mental health.

The Nintendo Wii allowed games to incorporate physical activity by swinging or moving the controller.

That kind of treatment is meant to help participants focus their attention on neutral targets by giving more weight to the neutral word or photograph than to the more aggressive one, with the hope that the patients will apply that line of thought to reality. A control group was formed as well, which had the participants do the same kinds of tests, but in that case the system determined whether the neutral or hostile word or image was targeted equally. The researchers found that this sort of treatment can also help people with anxiety and social phobias.

Other attempts to treat PTSD through video games have been made, such as the video game *Autumn* for the Oculus Rift virtual reality machine. The premise involves the aftermath of a sexual assault, particularly dealing with

Pokémon Go *is an "augmented reality" game because it shows virtual creatures in real-world settings on a smart phone or tablet. The game was immediately popular when released in 2016, with players of all ages getting out and walking around their neighborhoods trying to capture Pokémon creatures like the Nidoran, shown above.*

struggles relating to the world around the protagonist as well as herself. It was created by two Copenhagen-based students, Marta and Mikkel. *Autumn* has been described as a game that offers "glimpses into a character's journey during the months following a sexual assault: her struggles with herself and the world around her."[21] Because of its interactivity, the creators argue that it is a good way to evoke empathy in players, as well as to deliver human experiences to them.

VIDEO GAMES WORSEN PHYSICAL AND MENTAL HEALTH

The opposing arguments on this are rather obvious. While there have been a few video games that have promoted exercise directly or indirectly, most have little to no exercise benefit. Not only that, many games seem to encourage extended play, for example, through feedback loops, which are designed to keep people playing. Other games have no real end, such as *Tetris*, where players play until they lose, and then often have the urge to start "One more game...."

One study analyzed the increase in rates of **venous thromboembolism** due to a variety of factors, including a rise in obesity. The authors noted that obesity is an example

"To our knowledge, this study provides the strongest evidence for an independent association between time spent playing electronic games and childhood obesity.... Our findings suggest that the use of electronic games should be limited to prevent childhood obesity."[22]
—Dr. Nicolas Stettler, pediatric nutrition specialist

Studies have found that people tend to ingest more high-calorie foods when they play video games. This can lead to weight gain when a gamer doesn't exercise.

of an effect that could be reasonably curbed, and they discussed how it leads to a sedentary lifestyle and prolonged immobilization. They also noted excessive video game use as a factor in four children who suffered from venous thromboembolism. Persistent unmoderated video game play also has been shown to be associated with muscle pain, imagery that might cause seizures in photosensitive people, a lack of vitamin D from limited exposure to the sun, and sleep deprivation.

Video games have also been linked to an increase in calorie consumption. A study conducted by researchers at the Children's Hospital of Eastern Ontario Research Institute in Ottawa, Canada, found that the teenage male participants in the study felt more compelled to eat after they had played video games. The researchers speculated that it may be because of energy expenditure during video game play time, in addition to experiencing a mental-stress effect that caused them to eat more calories than they expended through playing. This study has similar results to other studies, which found that extended screen time caused people to become more overweight. The lead researcher, Jean-Philippe Chaput, also found that this occurred with prolonged computer work.

As video games have become increasingly popular, concerns over their effect on hand and wrist health have risen as well. Unsurprisingly, the repetitive actions of using a controller, keyboard, mouse, and other peripherals can have a harmful effect on one's hands and fingers, creating

Excessive gaming or computer use can result in carpal tunnel syndrome, a painful condition in the wrists that can cause permanent nerve damage if not treated.

a risk for osteoarthritis and carpal tunnel syndrome. That has resulted in people experiencing chronic pain symptoms in their joints at younger ages.

Video game addiction has been one of the biggest health controversies in gaming. When players can't pull themselves away from the experience, they are unable to care for themselves or others properly. The lack of self-control due to video game addiction can have fatal repercussions: In 2015, Hong Kong experienced at least two deaths due to exhaustion from playing video games for too long, including a man who passed away after a three-day-long gaming marathon at an internet cafe.

Recently, the video game *Fortnite* received a lot of controversy due to younger people playing the game to an excessive degree. It grew to be such a problem that it caused its publisher, Epic Games, to be sued. The plaintiff accused the company of not just making an addictive game, but actually designing the game using psychologists in order

A Nintendo employee demonstrates the Wii Fit U at the World Video Games Expo in Los Angeles.

to make it as addictive as possible. In 2019, video game addiction was classified as a mental illness by the World Health Organization, under the name of "gaming disorder." It is very important that parents monitor their kids' play, as while video games can have an addictive nature, someone who can step in and pull a child out of the loop is essential. That becomes more difficult when adults suffer, as they might not have someone to act as a countermeasure.

TEXT-DEPENDENT QUESTIONS

1. How much time, on average, do teenagers spend sitting in front of a screen?
2. What was the *Wii Fit*?
3. Name a reason why video games might be linked to greater calorie consumption.

 RESEARCH PROJECTS

The subject of video game addiction gets a lot of discussion, especially with how it has been classified in recent years. Some video games feature mechanisms designed to give players an incentive to cease playing, while others merely encourage them to take a break. Besides those discussed in this book, what are some examples of how video games try to discourage excessive play? What games include these features? Write a two-page paper.

WORDS TO UNDERSTAND

cryptozoology—the pseudoscientific study of beings who are not confirmed to exist (such as Bigfoot and the Loch Ness Monster).

genocide—the attempt, successful or not, to eliminate any group of people from existence. This can be done through killing or displacement, among other tactics.

political spectrum—a way of representing and comparing various political positions on a left (liberal) to right (conservative) scale.

stereotype—a widely held belief or image of people that is typically oversimplified.

DOES ENTERTAINMENT MEDIA HAVE EDUCATIONAL VALUE?

CHAPTER 4

Anytime that a young person is learning new things, there is a chance that they will come away from the experience with inaccurate or faulty information. When a person is not familiar with a topic, it can become that much easier to be misled by false information. As such, a society that increasingly exposes children to any kind of media will run the risk of teaching them the wrong lessons. Be it through YouTube videos that try to manipulate their viewers (or at the very least can be unintentionally manipulative), news programming that engages in biased reporting, or simply content that's distracting the media's audience from important things, there is a lot to worry about.

VIDEO GAMES AND OTHER MEDIA ARE USEFUL FOR EDUCATION

One of the benefits of video game interactivity is that games can help players develop certain skills. One commonly cited example involves the relationship between video games and driving skills. The 1989 Atari arcade game *Hard*

Drivin' was actually adapted for use in driver's training courses. More recently, a study by researchers from the University of Hong Kong and the Shanghai campus of New York University found that action-oriented video games can improve players' visuomotor control skills, which are used in driving. The researchers separated study participants into two groups, both consisting of nonvideo–game players. One group was tasked with playing and learning one of the titles in the more action-oriented *Mario Kart* racing game series,

Studies have shown that driving simulators and video games can improve real-life skills on the road.

while the other was tasked with playing and learning the roller coaster creation simulation video game *Roller Coaster Tycoon III*, which works at a more relaxed pace than *Mario Kart*. Members of both groups played their respective games for a combined ten hours across ten sessions. Once the sessions were complete, the participants were tasked with a driving simulation, with the objective being to drive down the center lane of a road while being affected by a crosswind. Another test required the participants to use a joystick to keep a floating dot at the center of the screen.

The results of the driving simulation showed that while the action-oriented players showed improvement in their visuomotor control skills, the other group showed no improvement. A secondary test that checked on the improvement after doing a similar setup with the first-person shooter video game *Unreal Tournament* found that action-oriented players showed improvement as well. In fact, Li Li, an associate professor of neural science and psychology at NYU Shanghai, and the study's lead author, noted that first-person shooting games can actually be more beneficial to driving ability than racing games, depending on what aspect of driving a person is trying to improve. Novice drivers would benefit more from racing games, while experienced drivers would benefit more from first-person shooters, Li suggests. "Our research shows that playing easily accessible action video games for as little as five hours can be a cost-effective tool to help people improve essential visuomotor-control skills used for driving," he said.[23]

Scan here to learn more about how stereotypes influence people.

Action games do more than just improve your reaction speed, however. They can also help improve a person's learning capacity. Games with a lot of details that a player must take into account, and with high stakes that need to be addressed accordingly, can help the brain anticipate a sequence of events. A recent study conducted by professor Daphne Bavelier, of the University of Geneva, used subjects who had little to no experience with playing video games, splitting the group into two. One group was tasked with playing first-person shooting games (such as *Call of Duty*), while the other group played nonaction strategy games (such as *The Sims*). Bavelier noted that the action-game players did not begin with a better template in mind for handling the situation than the other group did, but they were able to develop a template to better handle that situation. The study also showed a long-term increase in learning ability for the action-game players. However, the researchers were not entirely sure what aspect of action games caused that increase; they speculated that it may have been due to the fast-paced nature of the games or the need to anticipate things under pressure, which can be an element of nonaction games as well.

Games like Sid Meier's Civilization *may get students interested in history, but they are not necessarily going to help them pass their history tests. However, these games do help young people to develop critical thinking skills by requiring players to make important strategic decisions in order for their virtual civilizations to thrive. For example, they must weigh the pros and cons of engaging in conflict with their neighbors, as well as how to promote economic development and the well-being of their people in a way that is environmentally sustainable.*

Another type of educational inspiration that a child can get from video games is historical, with games like *Sid Meier's Civilization* or the *Age of Empires* series, giving players the opportunity to play as the leaders of various historical civilizations as they develop and expand their empires. For example, players can take control of Mahatma Gandhi of India, Gorgo of Sparta, or Cleopatra of Egypt in *Sid Meier's Civilization VI*, and they can get further insight into these people's histories. (These kinds of games serve as a good entry point, but for obvious reasons they should not be regarded as the be-all and end-all for a child's historical knowledge.) Another game that has become popular in recent years is the *Assassin's Creed* series, which is set in various points in history. Although the game has some ahistorical and alternate history concepts, it does a magnificent job of depicting ancient cities in fairly accurate ways. (*Assassin's Creed Odyssey* is considered to be a particular standout for its quality depiction of ancient Greece.)

Games can also introduce young people to religion and mythology. For example, the *Megaten* franchise is a series of Japanese games that features supernatural situations involving gods and demons from various religions (including Islam, Shintoism, Hinduism, Judaism, and Christianity), as well as Japanese mythology and **cryptozoology**. The *Kid Icarus* franchise is more cartoonish and lighthearted than the *Megaten* game, and features characters drawn from Greek mythology, such as Medusa, Hades, and Poseidon.

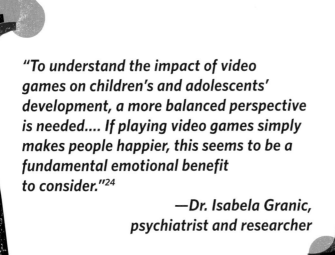

"To understand the impact of video games on children's and adolescents' development, a more balanced perspective is needed.... If playing video games simply makes people happier, this seems to be a fundamental emotional benefit to consider."[24]

—Dr. Isabela Granic,
psychiatrist and researcher

One of the earliest and most iconic educational video games is *Oregon Trail*, which was developed in the 1970s to teach kids about the journey that nineteenth-century pioneers took to the West. The game also helped them to develop and manage resources. Another famous game series that deals with history and geography is *Where in the World Is Carmen Sandiego?* That series of educational games, popular in the 1980s and 1990s, was both educational and entertaining. Players pursue the infamous thief Carmen Sandiego, who steals valuable objects. In order to find her and the objects, players must use clues found regarding Carmen's location and where she has been. The clues tie into geography so that they can learn about different locations as well as move on to the next area, hopefully one step closer to finding her. Variants of the game were released, including a history-based sequel called *Where in Time Is Carmen Sandiego?*, which involved time travel to different historical periods. The popularity of the game led to the release of related products in other media, including a television show for children.

Entertainment media such as movies, television shows, and video games can also be a great way to teach people about other cultures. The 2014 video game *Never Alone*, also known as *Kisima Inŋitchuŋa*, is a puzzle-platform game that is based on a traditional story of the Iñupiaq, an Alaskan

Playing games like Mario Kart can help improve a person's visuomotor skills, while simultaneously reducing stress and improving the player's mood.

group of Native Americans. The game was created through a partnership of the Cook Inlet Tribal Council and game publisher E-Line Media. The goal was to create a video game that could educate players about indigenous culture while also celebrating that culture. The game was developed for E-Line by Upper One Games—the first video game development company in the United States wholly owned by indigenous people. The creative director at E-Line Media, Sean Vesce, made a dozen trips to Alaska as part of his efforts to learn more about the culture, history, and values of the tribe while working on the game. "We were just blown away at the richness and the beauty and the depth of that storytelling tradition, and we realized that none of that had really been ever explored in a videogame," Vesce said.[25]

While *Never Alone* was meant to celebrate indigenous culture, other games exist to bring attention to suffering. The video game *Darfur Is Dying* was released in 2006 to cast a light on the suffering of refugees in the Darfur region of Sudan. At that time, there was a **genocide** occurring there. *Darfur Is Dying* was created by students from the University of Southern California. The goal of the game is to forage for water and survive, while playing characters of different ages and genders. The game teaches players how age and gender can affect a person's ability to survive hostile situations. It also includes a feature that sends a note to government leaders, requesting support for refugees from Darfur.

Logic games can also have educational purposes. Nintendo's *Brain Age: Train Your Brain in Minutes a Day!*

for the Nintendo DS was noted for its Sudoku, math, and writing puzzles. This game was created in cooperation with Ryuta Kawashima, a Japanese neuroscientist who was most notable for his book *Train Your Brain: 60 Days to a Better Brain*, which sold millions worldwide. The series has since had a number of entries, including miniature digital titles *Brain Age Express: Maths*; *Brain Age Express: Arts & Letters*; and *Brain Age Express: Sudoku*.

Another notable line of games is the *Professor Layton* series, inspired by a series of Japanese puzzle books called *Atama no Taisou*. The logic puzzles were integrated with a mystery story as well as an attractive European art style. They can help with critical thinking and managing multiple pieces of information, as failing to do so can make the game much more difficult to beat. The game's story helps to enhance these aspects of play.

ENTERTAINMENT MEDIA'S EFFECTS ARE OFTEN NEGATIVE

Over the past two decades, the line between entertainment and news media has become so blurred that many people can no longer tell the difference between the two. That has resulted in the rise of "fake news" that plagued the 2016 presidential election and beyond, where stories and memes were repeated on social media sites like Facebook, and even some that were obviously satirical were taken as the truth and reposted by some gullible citizens.

"The false idea that social justice causes have some sort of nefarious ulterior motive, that they're distorting the truth somehow [can help open viewers to more extreme cases].... Once you've gotten someone to believe that, you can actually go all the way to white supremacy fairly quickly."[26]

—Andrew,
former white nationalist

There is no easy way to solve the issue of fake news and media bias. Almost all news outlets have a leaning toward one side of the **political spectrum**, and their reports tend to be slanted in that direction. The political spectrum is a way of representing and comparing various political positions. In the United States, people who support policies that would restrict capitalism and redistribute wealth to provide greater opportunities for poor or underprivileged Americans are said to fall on the left side of the spectrum; they are sometimes called "liberals" or "progressives." Those who support the existing capitalist system and want lower taxes or a smaller government would fall on the right, or conservative, side of the spectrum. On this left-right scale, a person's views could range from moderate (or centrist) to extreme (at the far edges in either direction). The spectrum is not absolute—people can simultaneously hold views considered to be left-wing on some issues, while having right-wing attitudes on other issues.

Fox News is considered to be one of the more egregious examples of a right-wing bias, for both what panelists and hosts of its programs say as well as the kind of content the network allows to be shown. Independent observers have consistently found that Fox News reports are slanted toward the conservative, or right-wing, side of the political spectrum. On the other hand, publications like the *New York Times* and the *Washington Post* have a clear liberal bias, with stories slanted toward the left side of the political spectrum.

On both sides of the spectrum, the media tend to show certain biases and repeat **stereotypes** of racial minorities. For example, studies have found that crime suspects who are dark-skinned tend to be depicted in the media as more threatening than comparable white suspects are. Black suspects are more likely to be pictured in police custody or being physically restrained, more likely not to be identified publicly by name, and less likely to be depicted as well-dressed. Studies have also found that journalists are more likely to cover a story when the victim is white and the perpetrator Black, rather than the other way around. In one study, researchers found that when a news report played just a single sound bite, white people accused of a crime were twice as likely to be heard than Black people. When two or more sound bites were included in the news report, whites were almost five times as likely to be heard than Blacks. Additionally, the study found that it is extremely rare for a Black police officer to be featured on the news when the suspect is white, compared to a Black or white police officer featured in the case of a Black suspect.

One of the more pernicious examples of miseducation that children face comes from videos on online channels like YouTube. A person who records and posts a video does not need to prove their credentials, and as a result may

Fox News channel advertises itself as being "fair and balanced," but most independent media watchdog organizations consider the network's reports to fall on the conservative side of the political spectrum.

provide false or misleading information, either through incompetence or malice. One outlet that was criticized in this regard was the YouTube channel PragerU, which was created by a conservative talk show host and writer, Dennis Prager. The channel produced videos that sought to educate from a conservative viewpoint and were sometimes provocative. Critics noted that some videos opposed the scientific consensus on climate change or denied the existence of bias by police officers against Black Americans.

The algorithms that run social media sites like Facebook and Twitter, as well as sites like YouTube, tend to show people stories and video links about things they are interested in or produced from perspectives that they agree with. This has contributed to the problem of "fake news," where people repeat false stories because they agree with their worldview.

A related problem involves the algorithm that YouTube uses to show related content to users. There have been instances where watching an apolitical video might lead the viewer to be recommended content that is extreme, such as a video featuring white supremacists like Stefan Molyneux. Molyneux has been accused of being a cult leader and using cult indoctrination techniques, and he speaks in a way that makes him sound like an authority without actually doing academic research on his subjects. That gives viewers the impression that Molyneux knows more about the subject than he actually does. Not only can that mislead viewers into believing false information, it can also cause them to deny any notion that this information is false, because the author is so convincing.

There is also an issue when video makers veer off from their areas of expertise. For example, the atheist community on YouTube was originally focused more on promoting science and fighting religion, but in recent years some notable content creators in that community began to make antifeminist videos as well. Younger people who were interested in atheism became susceptible to the creators' antifeminist agenda. There is some dispute over whether the YouTube algorithm is responsible for the radicalization that some experience online, however. According to one study, many people who consume extremist content online were were already primed to fit the video makers' demographics when they clicked on the video.

Although there are a few video games that can be useful in educating players, most games fail at that task. That is either because of issues with the methodology that reduce or eliminate the value of the educational material, or because they simply are bad games, and thus the players will not feel incentivized to continue playing. Those kinds of games are a dime a dozen; some notable examples of bad educational games are the series of *Mario* educational video games, such as *Mario Is Missing!,* a geography game, or *Mario's Time Machine,* in which the characters travel through time to different historical periods and help various figures in their times. The problem with those games is not that they are controversial, because they are mostly inoffensive. It's that they are utterly boring, making it hard for kids to keep their attention on them. The games try to mash up traditional Mario and Luigi gameplay with educational gameplay, but manage neither aspect particularly well. As a result, there is little benefit from the sparse educational content.

A few other examples of bad educational video games include *Captain Novolin*, which is about healthy eating and diabetes, and *Bronkie*, which is about asthma. Both of these games originated from noble ideas, as they provide examples of how people deal with limiting conditions, and they impart good advice. The problems previously discussed about the *Mario* games are even worse in these cases, as *Captain Novolin* and *Bronkie* are downright awful, featuring terrible controls and gameplay. Designers of educational video games need to do better, because a lot of game designers provide the setup but fail on the payoff.

TEXT-DEPENDENT QUESTIONS

1. What are two benefits of action video games?

2. What video game took inspiration from the culture of the indigenous Iñupiaq people of Alaska?

3. What are the two sides of the political spectrum?

 # RESEARCH PROJECTS

Never Alone is well regarded for its educational content on the culture of its people, but it is just one of many games that explore cultures that may not have as much exposure as others. What is another video game that explores smaller cultures? Does the game do that well? Write a two-page paper.

WORDS TO UNDERSTAND

loot box—a video game object that players obtain, typically (though not always) for real-world currency or purchasable in-game currency, that contains random objects that are used in the game.

merch—slang for "merchandise," often referring to products like T-shirts or stickers that include a logo or slogan and are meant to advertise a person, brand, product, or event.

microtransaction—a type of purchase that can be made in a video game, exchanging real-world money for fancy outfits, better weapons, or other upgrades to the basic game experience.

DOES MEDIA MANIPULATE POSITIVELY OR NEGATIVELY?

CHAPTER 5

If there is one thing that children are, it's impressionable—they soak up all sorts of information rapidly. That impressionable nature, however, can also result in a child becoming addicted or spending large amounts of money on video games. Unchecked spending on **microtransactions** (in-game content sold in exchange for real-world money) has seen people increasingly spending money on games, to the point that the video game industry has taken to referring to particularly high or frequent spenders as "whales."

One particular issue the industry has faced in recent years is the **loot box** controversy. Loot boxes are objects, found in video games, that contain various items. These boxes are often purchased with either real-world money or an in-game currency (which itself can often be purchased using real-world money). In some games, the items can be purely cosmetic, such as an alternate costume or style for a character to wear. In other games, loot boxes can provide an advantage over other players.

Loot boxes have had an increasing presence in the video game industry, entering the mainstream in large part thanks to the 2016 video game *Overwatch*. However, the first known loot box in a video game appeared in 2007, in the free-to-play Chinese video game *ZT Online* released by Zhengtu Network. In China, where people did not have extra funds to spend on video games, many people were sharing games for free in internet cafes or using pirated versions.

Come to **Marlboro Country.**

An example of the manipulative power of media, Marlboro ads implied that people who smoked their cigarettes would be like the rugged Marlboro Man. According to the magazine Advertising Age, *the Marlboro Man and Ronald McDonald are among the most iconic advertising figures of the past half century.*

The game's developer added microtransactions to provide a way to monetize the game beyond the initial point of purchase. The approach proved to be successful and influenced many subsequent games.

Loot boxes manipulate people to make purchases in video games, in the same way that advertisements do in other media. But is this manipulation inherently bad, or is there a positive aspect to it as well? The following essays examine both sides of this question.

MEDIA IS NEGATIVELY MANIPULATIVE

Media has often carried a manipulative element, mainly in the form of advertisements. Advertising has taken many forms since the seventeenth and eighteenth centuries, when magazines and newspapers sought financing. Those publications began to work with businesses, offering them space to promote their products in exchange for money they could use to subsidize the cost of publication. Early advertisements typically were for books and for products with supposed medicinal effects. However, the differentiation between editorial content and ads is a problem that society has had to contend with for many years.

This mutually beneficial arrangement helped with the development of product branding. Because companies could get their specific names and products into people's consciousnesses through advertising, long-term success often became a matter of which brand could stand out the most. In the twentieth century, new forms of media were

> *"Teenagers today are in a seemingly unbreakable relationship with their phones, and (more importantly) the social media apps on which they communicate throughout the day and often well into the night. Any parent will know that most kids are so attached to their phone that the device almost seems welded to their hand much of the time. They are addicted and, as with any addiction, breaking the cycle of behavior is a complex, painful, but absolutely vital business."*[27]

> —*Jane Lunnon,*
> *school administrator*

created, such as radio, films, television, comic books, and, more recently, the internet. Advertising has followed on all of those platforms.

For many years, there was little regulation of advertisements. For example, until the 1960s, ads for cigarettes or other tobacco products could claim that smoking was healthy. Of course, the opposite is true—smoking is known to cause many health problems, including heart disease, breathing disorders, and different types of cancer. Cigarette ads were targeted to attract different demographics, and tobacco industry executives tried to undercut anti-tobacco lobbying. Even cartoons for children included advertisements for cigarettes during the 1960s. For example, a 1961 episode of *The Flintstones* included an ad that depicted Fred Flintstone and Barney Rubble smoking Winston cigarettes and talking about how they tasted good and were better than other brands.

More subtle issues with advertising that children may consume can be found in fast-food ads and commercials during children's broadcasting. There was a long-standing controversy over the use of Ronald McDonald and other child-friendly characters in association with the unhealthy food items that the fast-food chain sells. In 2011,

Jake Paul, one of YouTube's most controversial creators, has been criticized both for selling merch to children as well as for his explicit and dangerous antics in videos that are tagged "family friendly."

Shop

Diamonds | Packages | Special Offers

183 +20%
367 +44%
735 +70%

110
Diamonds

220
Diamonds

530
Diamonds

1250
Diamonds

Many gamers dislike microtransactions because they enable players who are willing to spend more money to have a better chance to win the games. For example, the diamonds in the online game Forge of Empires *can be used by players to purchase technology and buildings that can improve their cities. The purchase of "loot boxes" has been compared to gambling for children.*

more than 550 doctors called for the characters to be retired, claiming that their child-friendly nature influences children to want to eat at McDonald's, leading to weight gain and poor nutrition. "Stop making the next generation sick—retire Ronald and the rest of your junk-food marketing to kids," wrote Dr. Steven Rothschild, an associate professor of preventative medicine at Rush Medical College.[28]

There also has been an issue with YouTube content creators doing a poor job of distinguishing advertisements from their other content. That is a problem in a variety of media, but YouTube, being a relatively new medium, is unregulated and relatively unsupervised. Brothers Logan and Jake Paul are among the more problematic examples and have faced criticism for the amount of advertising they integrate into their content. One video by Jake Paul features a Christmas song that basically amounts to an ad, directly encouraging children to ask their parents to buy his **merch** ("Go tell your momma, she gotta buy it all"). That is obviously not good, as children are quite impressionable and largely unable to recognize the difference between content and advertising. One example of this is an incident where toys in a commercial morphed into animated versions of the toys. An uproar occurred as people criticized the advertisement for depicting the toys doing unrealistic things. Children actually thought the toys could turn animated in real life, as they did in the commercial. That may seem silly, but it shows how children's minds work and how susceptible children are to misleading advertisements.

When it comes to video games, proposals have been made for dealing with microtransactions and loot boxes. One that has gained some traction is to make it illegal to

To learn more about how advertisements manipulate people, scan here.

market video games that contain loot boxes to minors. Under that proposal, any game that features a loot box would have to be rated Adults Only (AO), an incredibly rare designation from the ESRB. That would significantly affect sales of the game, because major retailers like Walmart often refuse to sell AO-rated games. (That was the case with the controversial game *Grand Theft Auto: San Andreas*, which was designated AO until the publisher removed some inappropriate content.) If such an agreement were to be reached, it is likely that game publishers would create software patches that could eliminate the loot boxes so that they would still be acceptable for younger players.

Some of the most prominent examples of loot boxes and microtransactions occur in video games that are not themselves marketed toward children, though the M rating designation (17+) would still ensure that children under age eighteen would have legal access to games with that kind of content. Something that is more likely to raise ire among more groups, and increase the likelihood of politicians reaching across the aisle for resolution, is the presence of loot boxes and other microtransactions in video games meant to be played specifically by children. One such example is a Capcom-developed video game called *Smurfs Village*, where players cultivate a village for the Smurfs and can spend real-world money in order to do so.

While some loot boxes are less manipulative, others have received a particularly strong degree of criticism. Electronic Arts has faced its fair share of criticism for its implementation of loot boxes, particularly in *Star Wars: Battlefront 2*, where they were particularly troublesome due to not only the difficulty of obtaining content but also the content itself. Players actually had to get Darth Vader through the loot boxes or through experience, but the experience required was so high that it was not reasonable to expect players to get him as a character without paying for him first. EA tried to respond to that and fix the issue by lowering the amount of experience required to unlock Darth Vader, but that was largely invalidated because they also reduced the amount of

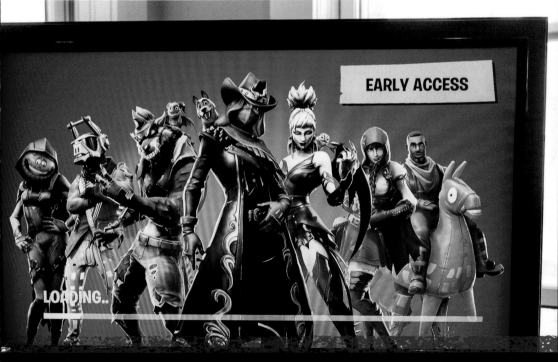

Although Fortnite *can be downloaded for free, players must purchase a $10 battle pass each season to participate in the popular Battle Royale format, and can spend additional money to upgrade their character's clothes ("skins"), weapons, and dances.* Fortnite *is the most profitable video game of all time, earning over $10 billion.*

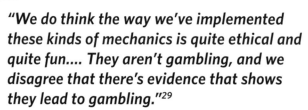

"We do think the way we've implemented these kinds of mechanics is quite ethical and quite fun.... They aren't gambling, and we disagree that there's evidence that shows they lead to gambling."[29]
—Kerry Hopkins, Electronic Arts vice president of legal and government affairs

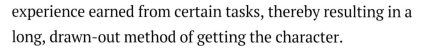

experience earned from certain tasks, thereby resulting in a long, drawn-out method of getting the character.

One deeply problematic area for microtransactions is mobile gaming. In recent years, mobile games have become a hotbed of manipulative tactics. One of the most common tactics is to implement a timer or currency that is spent in order to play levels. If either of these runs out, players have to wait until they recharge, or they can pay to have them recharged immediately. In certain games, that may not be too bad; the distinction between a good and bad example of this is really determined by consistency and generosity.

Having a financial means by which to progress in a game inherently preys upon a person's addictive personality, if they have one, and it only gets worse if the game is stingy about giving players the resources to play, has a time limit that is too short, or is designed in such a way that it begins to become more and more difficult to earn the currency or beat the levels, and therefore encourages the players to spend more than they would early on. Games that use such a system include *Fire Emblem: Heroes,* and *Candy Crush Saga. Candy Crush Saga* also has the issue of having the player lose more games than they win, and having items that a person can purchase with real-world money in order to give them an advantage. Dana Smith of *The Guardian* discussed how a big reason why people play *Candy Crush Saga* so much is due to the game causing players' brains to release dopamine whenever they win a level. The dopamine causes players to experience a happy sensation, but in turn, their brain will expect more. Thus, as levels in *Candy Crush Saga* begin to get harder and harder, the release of dopamine becomes less and less common. As a result, players may find themselves feeling more willing to open their wallets and pay up for the ability to get past a level or to continue playing sooner. The writer compared the feeling that people get from playing that game to the feeling they get when they play slot machines. It is unpredictable whether they will win, but that happens often enough that it remains satisfying to continue.

Another type of exploitative content in the mobile space is the "Gacha game." *Gacha* refers to the Japanese name for a capsule-toy vending machine. Those kinds of games can be any variety of genres: strategy, action, role-playing, sports, racing, what have you. The common thread among them is that the method by which players get content in the game is generally through a random vending system. *Fire Emblem: Heroes* is an example of a gacha game, where players have to obtain most of their characters through that system using a currency called "Orbs." The currency is acquired through playing the game normally and undertaking quests, but much like how *Candy Crush Saga* eventually gets more difficult, *Fire Emblem: Heroes'* Orbs become more scarce over time. That requires players to either exercise patience—which is exceedingly difficult if they enjoy the feeling of getting new characters—or pay money for more Orbs to buy more characters. The worst part of it is that if the players don't get a new character or even a character that they wanted, they may view it as a complete waste of time and money.

MEDIA CAN MANIPULATE IN POSITIVE WAYS

"Manipulative" is a word that is often used negatively. However, media can also manipulate in positive ways, which probably occurs more often than negative examples. For example, the 2009 Pixar film *Up*, about an older man who loses his wife and becomes obsessed with flying his house to his and his wife's dreamland, had many emotional highs and lows. One of the saddest scenes was a ten-minute-long montage of memories spanning most of the couple's life, which caused even the most macho of men to shed tears. The writers intentionally told their story in a way that was emotionally manipulative, making the viewing audience feel sad. In the same way, viewers can be made to feel other emotions. The Pixar studio has gained a reputation for pulling on people's emotions, with movies such as the *Toy Story* franchise, *Monsters, Inc.,* and *Finding Nemo*. Another Pixar film, *Inside Out,* actually personified the emotions that young people feel as they are entering the teen years: Joy, Sadness, Anger, Disgust, and Fear.

Media can also manipulate viewers for the purpose of giving them positive education. One of the most notable examples is the PBS show *Sesame Street,* which first aired in 1969. The creators of *Sesame Street* felt that one good way to educate children was to be able to grab their attention. It was programming meant to prepare kids for school, utilizing the fact that children are wont to imitate things on television in order to present them with educational material, such as words, numbers, and cultural concepts. The program also made a point of strictly modifying content to ensure that the secondary content (i.e., humor and educational material) did not interfere with the primary material.

For example, according to the book *Children and Television: Lessons Learned From Sesame Street,* some of the

The creators of Sesame Street *made a decision to influence young children in positive ways, helping them to feel good about themselves and showing them how to interact with others.*

Muppets were originally supposed to express their emotions in various slapstick ways, such as slamming their heads on the wall or falling backward. The creators decided that that took away from the message they wanted after research found that it did not promote good models of appropriate behavior. A character was also removed from the show after the creators determined that it exhibited negative racial stereotypes of Black people, which they feared would cause Black children to feel bad about themselves or cause non-Black children to internalize those negative stereotypes and affect their perception of Black people. The writers and researchers who worked on *Sesame Street* made a point of trying to zero in on exactly the kind of skills that the target demographic would most benefit from learning. As such, they strove to avoid talking about subjects that were already known by their viewers, or those that would be beyond their understanding.

Another significant example is *Mr. Rogers' Neighborhood*, which began airing nationally around the same time as *Sesame Street*. The show's host, Fred Rogers, was able to make his young viewers feel many different emotions, but he especially evoked comfort and love. People of all ages would tune in to watch a show structured around kindness and love, which were things that Rogers believed could help improve viewers' health. "My whole approach in broadcasting has always been, 'You are an important person just the way you are. You can make healthy decisions,'" Rogers explained in 1979. "Maybe I'm going on too long, but I just feel that anything that allows a person to be more active in the control of his or her life, in a healthy way, is important."[30]

In recent years, many people have begun to criticize social media for being manipulative and harmful, particularly to young people. However, recent studies have indicated that this is not necessarily the case. The studies, conducted at the University of Missouri School of Journalism, found that social media use did not impede the social well-being of participants. Other studies have found that for teenagers, social media can provide a beneficial connection to the outside world that extends beyond family members and friends. In fact, social media may offer the advantage of strengthening some relationships.

Most teens understand that social media networks manipulate users so that they will spend more time on their devices, according to a recent study by the organization Common Sense Media.[31] However, for them the trade-off is worth it. For many young people today, social media helps their communication with others by providing a medium through which they can express themselves. When words fail to convey a message, some people might prefer to send a message via social media. This provides an easy way to stay in touch rather than allowing relationships to fall to the wayside.

Additionally, children are less likely to experience feelings like isolation and detriments of cyberbullying when they also have the opportunity to develop friendships.[32] For some adolescents, offline relationships can flourish with the help of social media. Children who lack some social skills may learn appropriate interactions by talking with friends over text or instant messaging systems.

Social media use also improves the ability of teenagers to use technology. Information technology is a significant force in improved quality of life and economic growth. Building a future workforce consisting of adolescents who understand technology may improve a country's prospects for education, health care, energy, security, and other industries.

Researchers also believe that social media use may improve creativity of adolescents. Sharing art, music, writing, and other creative endeavors with both acquaintances and strangers has never been easier than on the internet. Adolescents can also develop their ideas through new creative media, like podcasts and blogs.

In addition to boosting creativity, social media may lead to an increase in critical thinking and problem-solving skills. When adolescents read social media posts, they often compare their own values to those of others. They may also benefit from the exposure to other ways of thinking. In a way, social media use may also work as an exploration into different schools of thought. Additionally, reading social media posts means that students may have to find new ways to support their own opinions after reading them online.

TEXT-DEPENDENT QUESTIONS

1. Which animated TV show was used to sell cigarettes?

2. Name an early example of a video game that included loot boxes.

3. When did magazine and newspaper advertisements begin to become more commonplace?

RESEARCH PROJECTS

Do you think social media is good or bad for social skills and mental health? Find three pieces of evidence supporting your opinion. Then find three facts that support the opposite viewpoint. Do these opposing viewpoints change your opinion? Write a short paper in which you explain why or why not.

cannabis—any of the various parts of the plant, especially the leaves and flowering tops, from which marijuana and similar hallucinogenic drugs are prepared.

closed circuit television (CCTV)—a system of televising by cable to designated viewing sets, like in an office building, as an aid to maintaining security.

censorship—examining various media for the purpose of suppressing parts that are deemed objectionable on moral, political, military, or other grounds.

controversy—a prolonged public dispute, debate, or argument concerning a matter of opinion.

desegregation—the elimination of laws or customs under which people from different religions, ancestries, ethnic groups, etc., are restricted to specific or separate public facilities, neighborhoods, schools, organizations, or the like.

enslave—to make a slave of, or hold someone in slavery or bondage.

Entertainment Software Rating Board (ESRB)—rating categories for video games which indicate age appropriateness.

facial recognition—technology that makes it possible for a computer to recognize a digital image of someone's face.

gateway—relating to an ingested substance, habit, activity, etc., that is relatively free of bad effects but may lead to more dangerous or extreme choices.

global economy—the economy of all humans of the world, including all economic activities that are conducted both within and between nations.

mass media—the means of communication that reaches large numbers of people in a short time, such as television, newspapers, magazines, and radio.

pandemic—a disease that is widespread throughout an entire country, continent, or the whole world.

quarantine—a strict isolation or lockdown imposed to prevent the spread of disease.

racism—a belief that differences among the various human racial groups determine cultural or individual achievement; the idea that one's own race is superior and has the right to dominate others or that a particular racial group is inferior to others.

recreational use—use of a drug or medicine for enjoyment rather than to treat a medical condition.

spin—knowingly providing a biased interpretation of an event to influence public opinion about some organization or public figure.

surveillance—continuous observation of a place, person, group, or ongoing activity in order to gather information.

watchdog—a person or organization responsible for making certain that companies obey particular standards and do not act illegally.

ORGANIZATIONS TO CONTACT

American Psychiatric Association
800 Maine Avenue, SW, Suite 900
Washington, D.C. 20024
Phone: (888) 357-7924
Website: http://www.apa.org

National Alliance on Mental Illness
3803 N. Fairfax Drive, Suite 100
Arlington, VA 22203
Phone: (703) 524-7600
Website: https://www.nami.org

World Health Organization
Avenue Appia 20
1211 Geneva
Phone: +41 22-7912111
Website: https://www.who.int/

Entertainment Software Association
601 Massachusetts Avenue, NW
Suite 300
Washington, D.C. 20001
Website: https://www.theesa.com/

Parents Television Council
707 Wilshire Boulevard, #2075
Los Angeles, CA 90017
Website: https://www.parentstv.org/

TV Parental Guidelines
Monitoring Board
P.O. Box 771
Washington, D.C. 20044
Phone: (202) 570-7776
Website: www.tvguidelines.org

FURTHER READING

Gareth Schott, *Violent Games: Rules, Realism and Effect*. London: Bloomsbury Publishing, 2016.

Michael Davis, *Street Gang: The Complete History of Sesame Street*. New York: Viking, 2008.

Patrick M. Markey and Christopher J. Ferguson, *Moral Combat: Why the War on Violent Video Games Is Wrong*. Dallas: BenBella Books, 2017.

Pete Etchells, *Lost in a Good Game: Why We Play Video Games and What They Can Do for Us*. London: Icon Books, 2019.

Steven L. Kent, *The Ultimate History of Video Games*. Roseville, Calif.: Prima Publishing, 2010.

INTERNET RESOURCES

https://www.fcc.gov/
The Federal Trade Commission (FTC) is responsible for regulating content
on radio and television.

http://www.theesa.com/
The Entertainment Software Association (ESA) represents and regulates the
video game industry.

https://www.motionpictures.org/
The Motion Picture Association of America (MPAA) regulates the film
industry and rates individual movies based on the violence and adult content
they contain.

https://www.esrb.org/
The Electronic Software Ratings Board (ESRB) handles the ratings of video
games based on their content.

https://ncac.org/issue/video-games
The National Coalition Against Censorship (NCAC) advocates for free speech
in media, including video games.

CHAPTER NOTES

1   Jane McGonigal, *Reality Is Broken: Why Games Make Us Better and How They Can Change the World* (New York: Penguin, 2011).

2   Barack Obama, quoted in Joel Taveras, "Obama: 'Congress Should Fund Research on the Effect Violent Videogames Have on Young Minds,'" *Dual Shockers* (January 16, 2013). https://www.dualshockers.com/obama-congress-should-fund-research-on-the-affect-violent-videogames-have-on-young-minds/

3   Jill Disis, "The Long History of Blaming Video Games for Mass Violence," CNN (March 8, 2018). https://money.cnn.com/2018/03/08/media/video-game-industry-white-house/index.html

4   Donald Trump, "Remarks by President Trump, Vice President Pence, and Bipartisan Members of Congress in Meeting on School and Community Safety," The White House (February 28, 2018). https://www.whitehouse.gov/briefings-statements/remarks-president-trump-vice-president-pence-bipartisan-members-congress-meeting-school-community-safety/

5   Federal Communications Commission, "Obscene, Indecent and Profane Broadcasts," (accessed March 2020). https://www.fcc.gov/consumers/guides/obscene-indecent-and-profane-broadcasts

6   Donald Trump, quoted in Andrew Whalen, "Trump Blamed Video Games for Parkland Shooting but His School Safety Commission Says Otherwise," *Newsweek* (December 19, 2018). https://www.newsweek.com/trump-school-safety-commission-recommendations-violent-video-games-school-1265261

7   Colin Campbell, "Do Violent Video Games Actually Reduce Real-World Crime?" *Polygon* (September 16, 2014). https://www.polygon.com/2014/9/12/6141515/do-violent-video-games-actually-reduce-real-world-crime

7   Craig Anderson and Wayne Warburton, "The Impact of Violent Video Games: An Overview," in W. Warburton and D. Braunstein, eds., *Growing Up Fast and Furious: Reviewing the Impacts of Violent and Sexualised Media on Children,* (Annandale, NSW, Australia: The Federation Press, 2016), pp. 56–84.

8   American Academy of Pediatrics, "Policy Statement on Virtual Violence," *Pediatrics* 138, no 2. (August 2016). https://pediatrics.aappublications.org/content/138/2/e20161298

9   Jack Thompson, quoted in "Who's the Bigger 'Bully?' School Board or Game Maker?" ZDNet Education (March 14, 2006). https://www.zdnet.com/article/whos-the-bigger-bully-school-board-or-game-maker/

10 Hamza Shaban, "Playing War: How the Military Uses Video Games," *The Atlantic* (October 10, 2013). https://www.theatlantic.com/technology/archive/2013/10/playing-war-how-the-military-uses-video-games/280486/

11 Jai Mediratta "Video Games Distort Realities of War," *The Daily Nebraskan* (November 9, 2012). http://www.dailynebraskan.com/opinion/mediratta-video-games-distort-realities-of-war/article_78ad7c56-2a1c-11e2-8d0d-001a4bcf6878.html

12 Michael Rich, "What Should I Know about Fortnite—Is it OK for Kids to Play?" Center on Media and Child Health (May 22, 2018). https://cmch.tv/what-should-i-know-about-fortnite-is-it-ok-for-kids-to-play/

13 Craig A. Anderson, "Violent Video Games: Myths, Facts, and Unanswered Questions," American Psychological Association (October 2003). https://www.apa.org/science/about/psa/2003/10/anderson

14 Patrick M. Markey, quoted in Linda Stein, "Vilanova Prof's Study: Video Games May Reduce Violence," *Delco Times* (October 1, 2014). https://www.delcotimes.com/news/villanova-prof-s-study-video-games-may-reduce-violence/article_78740cd0-9200-538a-950e-ffb9133d9808.html

15 Markey, quoted in Stein, "Villanova Prof's Study: Video Games May Reduce Violence."

16 Christopher J. Ferguson et al., "Letter to APA on Policy Statement on Violent Media," Stetson University (October 7, 2013). https://www.stetson.edu/today/2013/10/letter-to-apa-on-policy-statement-on-violent-media/

17 Markey, quoted in Stein, "Villanova Prof's Study: Video Games May Reduce Violence."

CHAPTER NOTES

[18] Christina Lelon, quoted in Joanna Clay, "Gaming and Physical Therapy Come Together for Unique Research in the U.S. and Beyond," *USC News* (November 15, 2017). https://news.usc.edu/131166/at-usc-gaming-and-health-come-together-and-physical-therapy-will-never-be-the-same/

[19] Cornell University, "Corrupted Blood Incident—A Not-So-Virtual Epidemic in a Virtual World," Networks course blog (November 26, 2016). https://blogs.cornell.edu/info2040/2016/11/28/corrupted-blood-incident-a-not-so-virtual-epidemic-in-a-virtual-world/

[20] Melissa Glim, "Praise for Video Games as PTSD Therapy," *MD Mag* (September 3, 2015). https://www.mdmag.com/medical-news/praise-for-video-games-as--ptsd-therapy

[21] Jess Joho, "Can a Video Game Help Rape Survivors?" *The Atlantic* (January 7, 2015). https://www.theatlantic.com/entertainment/archive/2015/01/treating-ptsd-with-the-oculus-rift/384262/

[22] Nicolas Stettler, quoted in Jennifer Warner, "Video Games, TV Double Childhood Obesity Risk," WebMD (July 2, 2004). https://www.webmd.com/parenting/news/20040702/video-games-tv-double-childhood-obesity-risk

[23] Isabela Granic, quoted in "Video Games Play May Provide Learning, Health, Social Benefits, Review Finds," American Psychological Association (November 25, 2013). https://www.apa.org/news/press/releases/2013/11/video-games

[24] Li Li, quoted in Chris Cantle, "Video Games Improve Driving, According to New Study," *The Drive* (July 26, 2016). https://www.thedrive.com/accelerator/4583/video-games-improve-driving-according-to-new-study&xid=17259,15700021,15700105,15700124,15700149, 15700168,15700173,15700186,15700201

[25] Sean Vesce, quoted in Heather Bryant, "Native Stories From Alaska Give Gamers Something To Play With," NPR (August 23, 2014). https://www.npr.org/sections/alltechconsidered/2014/08/23/342554915/native-stories-from-alaska-give-gamers-something-to-play-with

26 Kelly Weill, "How YouTube Built a Radicalization Machine for the Far-Right," *The Daily Beast* (December 7, 2018). https://www.thedailybeast.com/how-youtube-pulled-these-men-down-a-vortex-of-far-right-hate

27 Jane Lunnon, "Our Children Are Being Manipulated by Addictive Social Media and the Government Must Step In," *The Telegraph* (June 16, 2018). https://www.telegraph.co.uk/family/parenting/children-manipulated-addictive-social-media-government-must/

28 Steven Rothschild, quoted in Lindsay Goldwert, "Ronald McDonald Bad for Kids?" *New York Daily News* (May 19, 2011). https://www.nydailynews.com/life-style/eats/ronald-mcdonald-bad-kids-mcdonalds-hits-back-critics-calls-clown-ambassador-good-article-1.141877

29 Ana Diaz, "EA Calls Its Loot Boxes 'Surprise Mechanics,' Says They're Used Ethically," *Polygon* (June 21, 2019). https://www.polygon.com/2019/6/21/18691760/ea-vp-loot-boxes-surprise-mechanics-ethical-enjoyable

30 Fred Rogers, quoted in Richard Gunderman, "Mister Rogers' Message of Kindness Is Good for Your Health," *Salon* (June 11, 2018). https://www.salon.com/2018/06/11/mister-rogers-message-of-love-and-kindness-is-good-for-your-health_partner/

31 Common Sense Media, "Social Media, Social Life: Teens Reveal Their Experiences (2018)," (accessed January 3, 2019). https://www.commonsensemedia.org/research/social-media-social-life-2018

32 Society for Personality and Social Psychology, "Declining Loneliness Among American Teenagers," (accessed January 9, 2019). http://www.spsp.org/news-center/press-releases/declining-loneliness-among-american-teenagers

INDEX

INDEX

AUTHOR'S BIOGRAPHY AND CREDITS

ABOUT THE AUTHOR

Abby Bryn is a writer and editor in Minnesota. She has worked in various fields, particularly media work. She enjoys traveling, visiting parks and other nature attractions, playing video games and table games, communing with friends, politics, and cats.

PICTURE CREDITS